Planning a Birthday Party

written by Faye Bolton
illustrated by Barbara Day

This edition first published in the United States in 1997 by
MONDO Publishing
By arrangement with MULTIMEDIA INTERNATIONAL (UK) LTD

For information contact:
MONDO Publishing
One Plaza Road
Greenvale, New York 11548

Printed in Hong Kong

First Mondo printing, October 1996
96 97 98 99 00 01   9 8 7 6 5 4 3 2 1

ISBN 1-57255-188-7

Originally published in Australia in 1988 by Horwitz Publications Pty Ltd
Original development by Robert Andersen & Associates and Snowball Educational

Contents

Introduction

A birthday is a special day and may be celebrated by having a party. Birthday parties are lots of fun but it's a good idea to plan them carefully. This book will help you plan a successful birthday party or any other kind of party you want to have.

Things to plan are:
— sending invitations;
— food and drinks for the party;
— games to play;
— party decorations.

March

Sunday	Monday	Tuesday	Wednesday	Thursday	Friday	Saturday
	1	2	3	4 Write a guest list	5 Make invitations	6
7	8 Send invitations	9	10 Choose games	11 Buy balloons	12	13 Make masks
14	15 Make decorations	16 Buy small prizes for games	17	18 Get replies	19 Make some more decorations and place cards	20
21	22 Buy drinks & borrow extra glasses	23 Buy food except fruit and bread	24 •Buy fruit & bread •Prepare food •Decorate room	25 PARTY	26 Vacuum room •Return extra glasses	27
28	29 Send thank you cards	30	31			

Guest list

Find out how many guests you may invite
and then write a guest list.

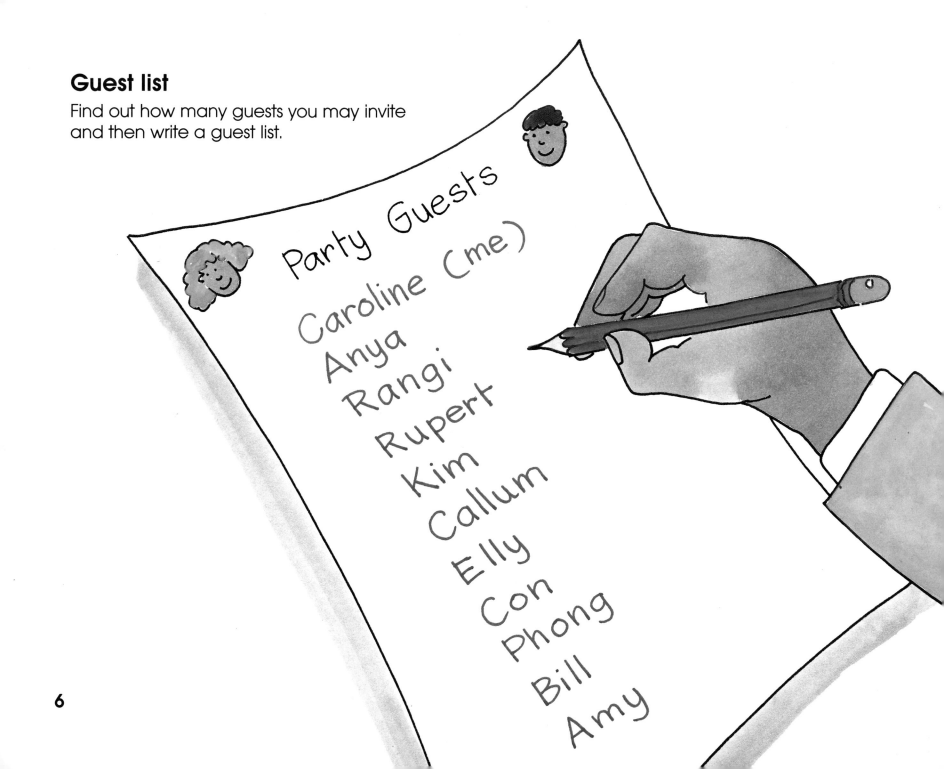

Party Guests

Caroline (me)
Anya
Rangi
Rupert
Kim
Callum
Elly
Con
Phong
Bill
Amy

Invitations

Make or buy invitations to send to your guests. Choose an interesting design and make sure the invitations fit into envelopes if they are to be mailed. Send the invitations approximately two weeks before the party.

Write your name, address, and telephone number on each invitation. Include the date of the party and the time the party begins and ends.

Food

Plan the food for the party. Party food is usually eaten with your fingers. It may include foods from around the world such as sandwiches, party pies and pasties, sausage rolls, mini hot dogs, pizza, potato or corn chips, fruit, and candy.

corn chips

party pies

← fruit

candy

sandwiches

pasties

pizza

sausage rolls

SAUCE

Tooth picks

paper napkins

potato chips

mini hot dogs

8

Sandwiches

Sandwiches can be made from many different types of bread. You could use rye, white, or whole wheat bread. You could also use pita bread, chappatis, tortillas, and matzos.

Chappati

tomato, coleslaw, and walnuts

salmon and cucumber on crisp bread

Tortilla

lettuce, tomato, and cheese

rye bread, salami, tomato, lettuce, and mayonnaise

Whole wheat bread, sardines, and lettuce

Pita bread, sprouts, carrot, cheese, and raisins

Matzo, gefilte fish, hard-boiled egg, and pickle

sub with celery, cheese, and raisins

9

Party pies and pasties

Party pies and pasties can be made with meat and vegetables. Some are made with cheese and spinach. They all taste delicious.

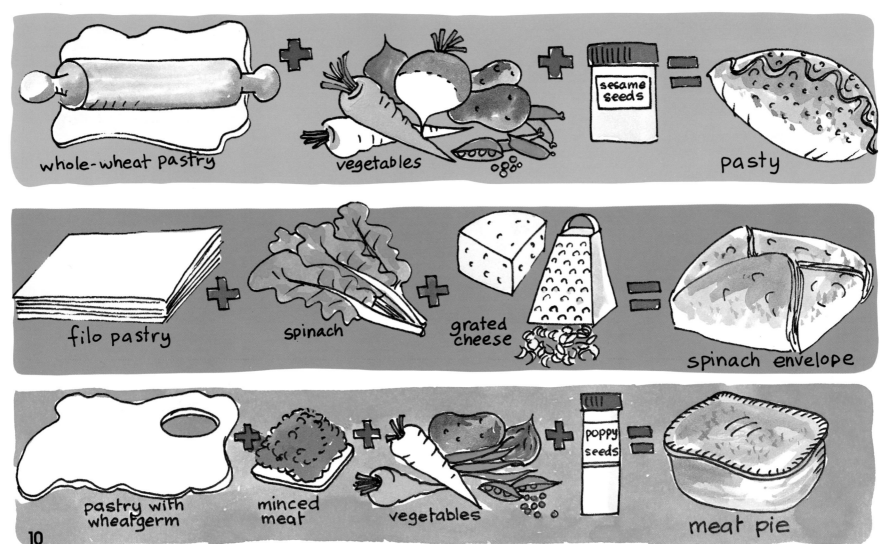

whole-wheat pastry + vegetables + sesame seeds = pasty

filo pastry + spinach + grated cheese = spinach envelope

pastry with wheatgerm + minced meat + vegetables + poppy seeds = meat pie

Novelty food

Novelty food is fun at a party. You may like to help make "Frogs in the Pond" using the following recipe.

Frogs in the Pond

This recipe makes twelve ponds.

Ingredients

- 3 boxes of lime Jello (to make ponds)
- 24 chocolate or gummi frogs
- 24 scoops of ice cream or frozen yogurt (to make water lilies)

What to do:

1 Make Jello by following the instructions on the boxes.

2 Pour the Jello into twelve bowls.

3 When Jello is nearly set, put two frogs on each pond.

4 Serve each pond with a scoop of ice cream or yogurt.

Novelty creatures

Novelty creatures are also fun to eat at a party. This is how you can make them. You will need:

cheese, apples, pineapple, radishes
slices of carrot and cucumber
raisins, nuts
licorice

pineapple rabbit

cheese mouse

radish robin

Kiwifruit and almond porcupine

cucumber crocodile with almond teeth

What to do:

1 Ask an adult to help you cut the cheese, fruit, or vegetable into the shape you need for the body of the creature.

2 Cut the slice of carrot or cucumber in half to form ears or wings.

3 Make a slit where the ears or wings will go.

4 Push the ears or wings into the body of the creature.

5 Add raisins and nuts to make the eyes, nose, and mouth.

6 Cut the licorice into thin strips and add it for whiskers and tails.

Birthday cakes

There are many different types of birthday cakes to choose from and they can be decorated in lots of different ways. You may like to help decorate your birthday cake.

chocolate cookies stuck into chocolate roll cake

Ice cream cake

Hedgehog cake

Clown cake

Rocket cake

14

Decorating birthday cakes

A round cake cut in half can be put together with a rectangular cake and decorated to make a birthday cake in the shape of a space station.

space station cake

A square cake and a rectangular cake can be put together and decorated to make a birthday cake in the shape of a computer screen and keyboard.

computer cake

15

Drinks

Allow about three drinks for each person at the party. The drinks might be fruit juice, pop, or punch. A special party drink is a fruit smoothie.

juice

ORANGE POP

Cola

punch

smoothie

16

Fruit smoothies

For each person you will need:

- a cupful of chopped fruit, such as banana, apple, pear, mango, peach, orange, or strawberry
- a cupful of fruit juice or mineral water

What to do:

1 Chill the fruit and fruit juice or mineral water.
2 Blend the fruit with the fruit juice or mineral water.
3 Pour into glasses and decorate.

Games

Choose the games to play at your party. Some favorites are Mexican Piñata, Pass the Package, Blind Man's Bluff, treasure hunts, and three-legged races.

Mexican Piñata

In this game, everyone takes a turn trying to break the piñata with a stick. When the piñata breaks, the dried fruit and candy fall out and everyone eats them.

You will need:

- a large balloon
- thin strips of newspaper
- scissors
- paste
- a shallow bowl
- masking tape
- decorations —
    - streamers, crepe paper, glitter, ribbon, buttons, and so on
- string
- dried fruits, nuts, and candy

What to do:

1 Blow up the balloon and tie it tightly.

2 Cut up newspaper into strips and cover with paste.

6 Then push the dried fruits, nuts, and candy into the opening.

7 Cover the opening with masking tape.

20

3 Cover all of the balloon with newspaper strips until there is a solid covering.

4 Leave the balloon to dry for a couple of days.

5 Ask an adult to help you cut a small hole at the base of the dry piñata.

8 Decorate the birthday piñata and hang it from a tree.

9 Everyone stands back behind a line.

10 Everyone takes a turn trying to break the piñata with a stick.

Pass the Package

To play Pass the Package you will need:
  a prize
  some smaller prizes
  lots of paper to make a big package
  a cassette recorder
  cassette tapes

cassette tapes

a cassette recorder

smaller prizes

STORY BOOK

READ ME

lots of paper

a prize

22

What to do:

Before the party
1. Wrap the main prize in paper.
2. Add layers of paper and small prizes until the package is big enough.

During the party
1. Seat guests in a circle.
2. Tell guests that they are to pass the package to each other around the circle while the music is played.
3. Play the music. Then stop it suddenly. Whoever has the package unwraps a layer of paper. If a prize is unwrapped, the guest keeps it.
4. The package is passed around as soon as the music starts again.

A variation of this game is to have only one prize in the middle of the package.

Make sure you have plenty of paper, pencils, felt pens, scissors, tape, and pins available for other games that the guests might suggest. Also have a cassette player with tapes, and perhaps have some small prizes available for the winners.

Decorations

Decorate the party area with balloons, crepe paper, and colored streamers. Arrange the furniture in the area and set the table. Set a plate, mug or glass, and paper napkin for each guest.

Place some balloons on your front door or front gate to let your guests know where the party is.

Party hats, place cards, and masks

Provide party hats and place cards for each guest and put them on the table. You may like to make these. If you have time you may also like to make some masks for your guests.

Making party hats

You will need:
    crepe or construction paper
    tape or stapler
What to do:
1 Cut wide strips of crepe or construction paper long enough to go around a head.
2 Join the two ends of each strip to make a circle.
3 Cut the top edge into points or fringe the edge.

Here are some other hats you could make.

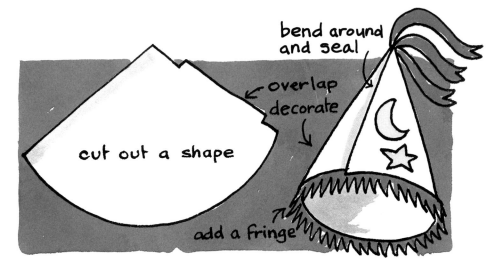

cut out a shape

bend around and seal

overlap decorate

add a fringe

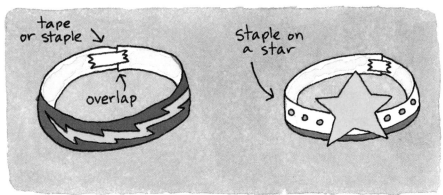

tape or staple

overlap

Staple on a star

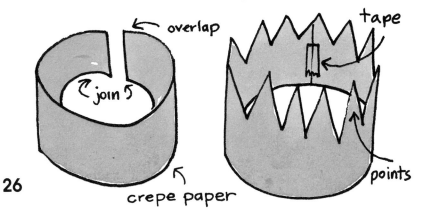

overlap

join

crepe paper

tape

points

paper bag

decorate

26

Making place cards

You will need:
- cardboard
- scissors
- felt pens

What to do:

1 Cut the cardboard to the size you want.

2 Fold the cardboard in half lengthwise.

fold

3 Write each guest's name on a folded card and decorate it.

Bill

Here are some other place cards you could make.

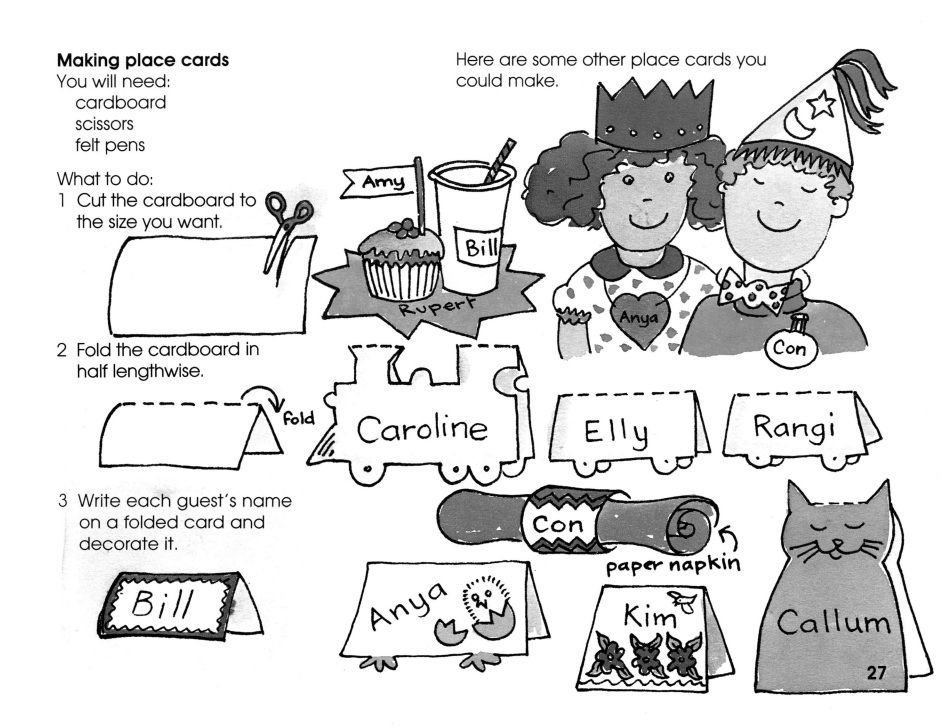

Amy

Bill

Rupert

Anya

Con

Caroline

Elly

Rangi

Con

paper napkin

Anya

Kim

Callum

27

Making masks

You will need:

    thin cardboard, wrapping paper, or foil
    decorations such as streamers, ribbons,
      lace, fake fur, buttons
    felt pens, scissors, tape, glue
    elastic

What to do:

1 Fold the cardboard, paper,
  or foil in half and draw the
  outline of one side of a
  face.
2 Leave folded and cut
  out the face.

3 Open mask and place
  over your face, with the
  central fold over your
  nose.
4 Carefully mark the
  positions of the eyes,
  nose, and mouth.

5 Remove mask and
  make holes for the eyes,
  nose, and mouth.
6 Decorate mask.
7 Attach elastic.

28

Arrival of guests

When your guests arrive, welcome them and take them to the party area. Introduce them to other guests they don't know and show them the areas that they can play in.

Party time
Have a wonderful party!

HAPPY BIRTHDAY CAROLINE

30

Cleaning up

When the party is over, say good-bye to your guests. You may like to give them a slice of birthday cake and a small basket of treats to take home. When the last guest has left, help clean up.

Index